GW01606269

ICONS

OF

TIME

AN EXPERIMENT IN AUTOBIOGRAPHY

Peter Abbs

For Barbara

ICONS OF TIME

First published by

The Gryphon Press
38 Prince Edwards Road
Lewes, East Sussex
BN7 1BE

ISBN 0 907137 04 0

Produced by Words and Images, Speldhurst,
Tunbridge Wells, Kent. TN3 0LH

Published with the support of Forward Publishing
4/7 Great Pulteney Street, London W1R 3DF

CONTENTS

AFFAIRS OF THE HEART

MOVING OUT

I

PROLOGUE

I have searched for myself.
Heraclitus

I

A Cosmic Story

And now, feeling querulous, God said 'Let
There be consciousness'. And slept. And out
Of his long dream confused man stepped.
Scorched victim of divine fission.
Crazed animal dipped into time.
And under the mushrooming cloud and through
The black snow crept towards the crime
Of his history, immolating his own kind -
For there was this burn and ache in his side
Which nothing, for long, could assuage or cool.
Nor could he recognise that darker face,
Reflected back from the cracked world's pool.
And God woke from his dream. And half-understood.
Sensed the nails through the palms. And the chafing wood.

II

Returning to Sheringham

I walk the promenade. Half-familiar faces
Drift past me, so much less monumental
Than I remember, so badly cracked. And faded.
In their canvas tents the same women
Sit. Still. Knitting. Staring out.
A brackish wind blisters the day. I go
Up the steps to our old house - how it
Has shrunk! Under the salt-laden breeze paint
Has peeled. Black cracks in the wood are deeper.
Hedge and gate have been wrenched out to make
A parking space. Now only a summer-house -
Vacant half the year. How did we ever
Live here cocooned is such a claustrophobic place?
Across geometric lawns unknown children shout.

III

Waiting for the Harvester

Here I stood in the crew-cut stubble,
Sharp stone in hand waiting for the harvester
To turn upon the final strip of wheat,
To see the hares dart wide-eyed into the gun's
Explosion or rise like crimson rags upon
The blades. Now, near the same spot I can
Hardly recognise the self I was;
Now I am no longer armed - I move
Across the earth, mesmerised; myself
Trapped in the last small track of wilderness.
At every footfall, at every dog bark,
Every quiver of the vast machine, I shudder.
Sense in my flesh my own sharp stone;
The damp blades whirring above dry bone.

IV

A Further Visit: February 1990

For my Mother

Back - and at each glance the town contracts.
How dwarf the buildings seem that once towered
Over me. All close-ups then; and sticky palms.
We take the bitter route along the promenade.
You talk of the latest deaths, lives slowly
Extinguished, last words said. At each return
There are further casualties to add. The sea
Is out; the iron defences bleed an oxide red.
At the cemetery we clear the grave. You plant
A rose. I touch the stone, sense Father's back;
White. Emaciated. Cold. A frenzied wind
Tears at our throats. The driven clouds blacken
The sun. I kiss you from the moving train.
The scene blurs behind me. It begins to rain.

V

Absence

I have been here before, chest pressed
Against the stone's worn ledge, feeling the same
Unease as I do now, peering through the gloom
And silence to the abrupt stop of water.
Through the darkening clouds, criss-cross of boughs,
My face stares back. Mouth bearded, wrinkled brows.
An actor's mask whose parts I do not recognise,
Whose lines I can no longer read. Hamlet
Without an audience? More like Narcissus -
Only myself here, under alternating focus.
What did I, a child, throw down this well?
A gap exists where the syntax ends.
There's a numbing sense of loss. Nothing
Comes back. This silence where these shadows toss.

VI

Who I am

He did not observe that with all his efforts he made no advance - meeting no resistance that might, as it were, serve as a support upon which he could take a stand, to which he could apply his powers, and so set his understanding in motion.

Kant

What is it that I do? This dizzy spinning
Of myself. This geometric cobweb that I make
From my own entrails. Intractable substance,
Obsessively shaped to a fine thread.
Part fact. Part fabulation. An obscure agent
In me fashioning the dark strands into pattern.
A design, somehow redemptive, however difficult.
What was could not have been otherwise.
There's a kind of freedom in admitting it.
Facts are weights. They tether random flight,
The delusions of Icarus, the Romantic type.
Filament by filament, inch by inch, I make
This architecture: a bound and limited life.
What I have struggled with is who I am.

II

FRAGMENTS FROM A CATHOLIC CHILDHOOD

'I rhyme
To see myself to set the darkness echoing'
Seamus Heaney

I

Premature Birth

Surname: Abbs. First names: Peter Francis.
Date of birth: 22.2.42. Place: Cromer.
The facts console. Deceive and mesmerize.
Yet mother's story has a nightmare ring.
All the way to the theatre she had screamed:
I want to die, I want to die, I want -
Until the gas took over. Born premature -
Cut from the womb three months too soon -
I choked into the commotion of hands, the glare
Of swivelling lights, muffled blare of plenitude.
Mother sighed *A girl? A girl?* and bitter, wept.
For her: scars from the surgeon's knife.
For me: slow, impeded waking into life.

II

At the Oak Woods

This morning, not as it usually is.
Not box-hedge, nor black currant, nor mint's aroma.
Merely the breeze tapping the window pane -
And Grandmother's there. With pins, with clips, she plaits
Her hair. Grandfather's sipping tea from his saucer.
I've slipped the intervening years again.
On the fire branches froth, sizzle, blaze, smoulder.
The varnished chairs shimmer like manufactured glass,
Their curving legs are tongues of fire.
I go down the green passage to the open door,
Splinters of God lie in the melting grass.
The marigolds stand erect; orange and oracular.
I go through the walled garden to the pond.
A goldfish surfaces. Circles. And is gone.

III

In the Woodshed

In the corner of the garden was the shed.
Across the door a fig tree arched, and spread.
Warmed by the sun its ribbed fruit hung down;
A ripe purple stained the outer rind.
Yet the palmate leaves were hands prohibitive;
They joined to shut one out. When pushed,
The door swung open. Inside it was illicit
Dark. Chill underground. I paused - time passed -
Then tiptoed down. Slowly **they** materialized:
In a corner kindling limbs were stacked and bound.
Serrated teeth gleamed from each black side.
A hacked torso rose up from the ground.

A nightmare rides rough-shod upon my sleep.
I was in too far. And down too deep.

IV

Unread Signs

Earth was littered with signs we did not read
Nor comprehend. In gaping pits we picked
Glossy blackberries or collected from the ground
Cold metal shapes, long, tapered, with frilled edges
Chock-full with grit and sand. Harder than shale
Whatever force had forged them, they were made to last.
Blankly we accepted them, bits from dislodged turf,
Fragments of the sliding screes we tried to scale.
Barbed wire poked through bramble thickets
Or dangled, flaking, from the cliff's ledges.
We dived into a labyrinth of tunnels
Rank with urine and discarded papers:
Shells exploded, ships sank, burning cities fell -
We hurtled through the black; blind, ephemeral.

V

The Look-out Tower in the Oak Woods

We saw only what our guileless games allowed;
Assumed the shelter's womb led towards
The light. Always summer. The sea a sheet
Of wrinkled blue (on blue) with puffs of cloud;
No shadows ran along the silent beach -
Norfolk's backdrop to our blindfold play.
In the Oak Woods we climbed the look-out tower.
We leapt the missing steps. From the broken top
We watched the yellow squares streaked with scarlet
End abruptly with the shore. Low tide.
Stranded on the white chalk bed, a mine
Stared back at us with one blank eye.
But we stood up high, salt on our lips and brow,
Safe on the rotting planks - the moment, always now.

VI

Myrtle Cottage at West Runton

The West Runton Abbs were Methodists.
They ate meat on Fridays, placed no crucifixes
On the mantelpiece, read *Pilgrim's*
Progress and *The Methodist Recorder. Papists*
Grandmother spits out the word like it burns
Her mouth. Grandfather keeps himself apart.
Where the coast road turns to Roman Camp
He sits on the village bench. And talks Socialism.
I don't believe in any God you dress
Up for, he says. *And read between the lines!*
All his life he laboured for the genteel classes
He most despised. In Myrtle Cottage
A wood fire glows. Dark above the old bureau
An antlered stag stands high, where water flows.

VII

The Other Child

I look through the window of my first school:
St Josephs. R. C. Sheringham. Norfolk.
Through the pane of fractured glass I stare
Into that silent chamber, sunk from mind.
Silver radiators still stand by the dark green
But all the trappings - abacus, globe,
Charts, blackboard, maps - have long since gone.
Was I ever here? Learning God by rote?
Obscure eel in the shallow tank of learning -
Even then forgetful of names, dates, facts.
I cannot find the child I was. Nothing
Coheres. Or coincides. Or rhymes.
The school door's locked; the place is out of bounds.
A pensive boy inside does not turn round.

VIII

St Peter's College for Catholic Vocations: 1954

I mourn the child I seldom was. Precarious
At birth. Washed up, at last. At St Peter's
College. Freshfields. Liverpool. A pale
Face elongated with piety. Alabaster
Hands clutching the plastic beads. Or clasped
Before the fourteen Stations of the Cross.
Baroque actor straining to shed the child
Who seldom was. Who cried himself to sleep
While the Mill-Hill fathers' red sashed cassocks
Cracked and slapped against our wooden cells.
And priests in black gowns were walking their rounds
And binding with briars my joys and desires.

Dear child, I would tell you if I could. . . . .

A stricken deer makes for the shadowed wood.

IX

The Eczema of Christ

I remember your raw hands, first. And now
I see your face. Scored red. And white with flaking.
The eczema of Christ! And your name? What was
your name?
Was it Bailey? Slowly you said something
Like: *Go to the Loaches . . . . . It's the best place.*
It stank of excrement. But you were right.
The blocked homesickness streamed down my face.
That night I watched the Liverpool-Southport
Trains glide by. Each lonely passenger glowed
With a freedom I conferred upon them.
Mundane life - that lost beatitude!
On Friday nights we confess on bended knees.
We scour our soiled imagination clean.
A sick Christ dangles from the plastic beads.

X

An Undelivered Letter

Oh, but Christ, you were hooked on prayer.
Your cocaine rosary, your litany of valium,
Your cheap narcotics always at hand,
Available whenever the going got rough -
Or our exams came. Hunched in the church,
Small hands barricading your face, lips
Pursed up against the world's violation.
All that sacrifice! All those prayers! -
As the day-trippers mobbed past outside.
We felt we could not turn Cliff Road
Without the intercession of the saints.
And I, ham actor, sick to please
Tried to outstrip the illustrious saints for years,
Addicted to the dark, violet, heart-shaped words.

XI

The Death of Grandmother 1960

I was eighteen when Grandmother died.
She had fainted at the Catholic fete.
Was deep in a coma when we reached her side.
She recognised none of us.

Our agitated words sink into silence.
Your face hangs a crumpled mask come loose;
Somewhere your life edges into blackness;
The beads I give you dangle like a noose.

And she who filled our lives with so much talk
Died alone without a single word.
I look at you now in your wedding photograph;
Demure. More beautiful than I remember:

Any second your mouth will burst into a smile.
Your animal eyes hungry for their future.

XII

In the Museum

Unceremoniously they lay that ancient
Body out, unwrap the limbs. One by one,
Peel back the binding resin rinds.
With scalpels cut the pad of chaff and mud.
They number every bone. Brush, weigh and pack
The crumbling aromatic dust; unstring
The pious tags and take the last frail sheaves
Of faith, centuries of hope, dissolving.
Yet what do these masked surgeons work
To find under the scents and gnostic tricks
Of Anubis? Naked on the block
A human mortal lies: H7386;

Her hollow head, tilted back, rapacious
Mouth open, still gagging on the nothingness.

XIII

The Loss of Faith

What did we do when we unchained the earth from its sun?
... Are we not plunging continually?
... Are we not straying as through an infinite nothing?
Nietzsche

Who put the neon-lighting of his childhood
Out? A juke box throbs with *Jail House Rock*.
He reads Karl Marx and dreams of freedom.
He smooths his hair with daubs of Brylcream.
Gone from the Eucharist, where is God?
On Sheringham sands *I can connect nothing*
With nothing. The spray lashes into the dark.
In my own town I have become a stranger.
I kneel and pray before the blessed virgin -
My mind's a stew where Magdalene strips.
I enquire of all that lives its final aim.
The ornate dome of faith cracks and splits.
God created the world *ex nihilo*. And withdrew.
Then, one day, the nothingness seeped through.

III

FATHER AND SON

Spirit gains its truth only by finding itself in absolute dismemberment

Hegel

I

Tongue-tied

Father, now when I speak, I speak for you.
The silence you maintained could not be kept.
A knife, it spliced our mutual lives in two.
Tongue-tied, we were forever awkward. And inept.
Silence was our dumb inheritance.
The suicidal note passed down to us:
Keep your tongue still. Keep your mouth shut -
Numbing contract of our rural class.
The laconic words were slowly drawled
To dam our thoughts and let the feelings pass.
Nothing. Say nothing. Say nothing at all.
The anger mounting in the throat was swallowed back;
And swallowed back it became all hell to know
What the dumb thing was which choked us so.

II

Confidence in Speaking

In your wardrobe there were some pamphlets;
Their covers were crimson, the paper textured. *Smart,*
Mother would have said, with their striding titles:
CONFIDENCE IN SPEAKING IN TEN EASY PARTS.
But for us there was to be little confidence.
No public. No easy parts. The blade of silence
Axed whatever lived between us. *Life's*
A fucking swindle if you ask me, you said once.
But I didn't really ask. So the years passed.
Quietly they incinerated themselves.
Unremarked those crimson invitations
Disappeared. Tonight, because you're ill, I phone.
We cannot find the words we need, our speaking parts.
Our voices falter. That age-old silence starts.

III

Language!

Father, what was it which divided us?
It crawled without a name. It grew in our
Embarassment. A freak. An albatross
Worn privately. Yet it came from a power
Outside. *The 44 Education Act. The new welfare.*
This weekly drama comes drifting back.

My brother has returned from Paston School.
He does his language home-work in the parlour;
Declines regular nouns, corrects bad grammar.
Father, you scan *The Mirror* on the kitchen stool:
Jesus Christ! The bitch went down! Bloody Hell!
Fucked up m'bleedin Vernon's Pools as well!

Language! Language! Language! I hear my mother gasp.
The curtains hang like iron across the glass.

IV

Generations of Farm Hands

A metal sky weighs upon the horizontal land,
Drained, dyked, undemonstrative.
After all these years, I work to understand:
Give the silence a voice, the resentment tongue,
To brand it indelible on the fugitive mind.
Where did it begin, that subterranean anger,
Smouldering, barely exploding, quickly subsiding?
Chill ash. The lava of embarassment.
Was it being born rural working-class?
Generations of farmhands, time out of mind,
Forcing their feelings down till they drowned
To resurrect, embittered, against their own kind.
Civilization's dismemberment of man. Not hearts.
Not heads. Not tongues. But hands, severed hands.

V

Predicament

Father, what was it made us quell our convictions?
Tame our moving tongues? We had no politics.
No public thoughts. Our feelings became convicts
Without right of expression. Tortured by shame
They couldn't announce themselves in the boisterous
Square nor exonerate their names.
We hadn't the heart to claim the beauty of anger.
The pride of justice. Whatever truth stirred
In our shallow lives we hammered down.
Daily, we slew our aspiring selves and deemed
It wise. *Well, who the fuck does he think he is?*
Too clever by half!
Cut him down to size!
Yet all the time the bitter sea spoke otherwise.

VI

Written in Guilt

Father, even before the cards were cut,
Shuffled and dealt you said: *Count me out.*
At Mass your mouth shut tight as a clam
You crawled up the side-aisle to your god,
As if communion was all presumption
On your part or, more like, some *fucking sham.*
I analysed your christian gestures with an adolescent
Eye which had become, by then, savagely
Unchristian. Father, why did you have to go
Leaving not one sign, not one memento?
What was it jammed the body's flow?
You looked on, spectral, awkward, half-ashamed,
And craved extinction years before it came.

And who can forgive me now for saying so?

VII

After Retirement

And so, your retirement came. A short speech.
A drink or two. A few quid in an envelope.
Then there was no more spiel - or tips.
No further excursions billed MYSTERY TRIPS.
At night as the ecstatic sagas flowed
You crouched coughing up gobbets of phlegm.
Death sat sour on the grave of your tongue
And in a claustrophobic room with flowers
Time's demolitions haunted you. The decades,
Years, months, weeks, days, hours
Dissolved to this consuming now - to disappear.
Beyond the mock-Tudor windows could you hear
The despotic sea, wind perpetual, drift of things?
The stopped clock, clogged, under tidal sands.

VIII

Winter Visit

Day staggers in, glazed-eyed, an invalid.
Morning contracts to shrunken appetites.
Little endures that interests you much.
Something like tears slide down the glass.
Your allotment, hard won, reverts to wilderness.
The fertile square is now couch grass.
Downstairs the chiming clock conveys a measured
Sense of things, not our snapped thread
Where beads in darkness scatter out of reach -
Under the silent bed. Under the silent past.
Nothing culminates. I walk the beach -
The Bingo's boarded up, the glass pane's smashed.
I sidle the length of my childhood cage.
An empty bench observes the breaking waves.

IX

A Conversation with the Doctor at the Time of the Chernobyl Disaster

You stand at the window in your striped pyjamas,
Like a disaster victim, and I am outside.
It is the second of May. The hawthorn blossom
Froths and blows all over Sheringham.
The doctor takes me to his car and says:
Your father hasn't much longer to go.
Over our heads the arctic clouds explode.
And mushroom. *He has the worst heart I know.*
The wind, unseen, plucks at our hair and clothes.
He is living on borrowed time. And pills.
I catch you at the window waiting for news.
There is nothing, nothing more medicine can do.

You turn to me, taciturn: *What did he say?*
And all about us spreads cancerous May.

X

Crisis

As a child destroys a toy it has become
Indifferent to, so nature has it in for you.
Once partisan, now it doesn't care a jot;
It knows precisely where, when, how you'll crack.
The plastic bottles untidy the tidy house.
You swallow pills for urine, pills for gout,
Pills for sleep and now tranquillisers to ease
The dying. For two days they knock you out.
You drift among us, neither living nor dead.
Then the waves of pain come surging back;
They break over your hallucinating head.
All night you drown for want of common breath.
Day washes up the mess. Nothing's to be done.
A holocaust sky blots out the sun.

XI

November Garden

This November's slow. An aging sun weeps cold
On stone. You remain an invalid in bed.
Your body's shrunk. You lie small as a child.
I won't fucking mend this time, you said.
Your mind meanders through a maze its own.
The clinical air blasts my face and head.
And all you want is to be left alone.

This garden's become a place I almost dread.
A rectangle of smoking foliage. More gaps
Than substance. What fruit remains is cut and hollow.
The weight of barren years drags down my steps.
I recall early frosts, the drifting snow,
Snow that, once, as we walked, filled in our tracks -
Snow that was always driving in, behind our backs.

XII

Other Memories

Father, I've been unjust to you.
Less than fair. Large with my own self.
Janus, the two-faced god, is always true;
There were other times. We had other selves.
Now I remember how in slippers you padded
To our room, to turn out the gas light.
The small gashed globe went ember-red
And briefly smouldered on into the night.
As the purring faded our room regained
Its attic silence. And then you quietly came
To both our sides. You made the sign of Christ
Upon our sleepy heads. And said 'God bless'.
Now in the greater darkness, the small light out,
Your clumsy silent hands seem, almost, eloquent.

XIII

Requiescat in Pace

Words on the gravestone of Eric Charles Abbs

When we saw your body laid out, decked
By mortician's hands, mother kissed your lips -
As if you were breathing still - and merely slept.
But I sensed, most of all, an absence.
Your head was arranged like an effigy
In wax. Life-like - yet unlike you. So cold
To touch! Finally, you'd gone.
Two years have passed.
I catch sight of you now in glinting mirrors.
In my own feelings identify your quirks of soul:
Restless. On edge. Depressed. Equivocal.
Nature's both angel and born terrorist.
She slaughters to continue. The self's like breath -
Ephemeral. Yet I'll find words for both of us.
Make poetry break and bear the silence.
Requiescat in pace.

XIV

FF11506 Driver

Those who suffer in silence know no history.
Plato had a metaphor for it. Blindness,
Passivity of mind. He put us underground,
Hunched prisoners of the dark, watching dark
Shadows cast upon the dark. Exiled from the sun.
An absence of light. And no clear lineage.
Given the tabloid version, the TV image.
The cavern's shadows were always on the screen.
We'd no idea of who we were or who we'd been.
We went ashamed of what was rightly ours.
When relations died we burnt their personal things.
The photographs melted in the ash like tears.

Today I come across your driver's badge;
I grab it like a kleptomaniac.

XV

The Singing Head

Harsh. And remote. A square for graves.
A mile from Sheringham. The coast road.
Wind warps the hawthorn. Dwarfs the pines.
Brine abruptly burns the memorial rose.
Mother mourns here, planting against the odds.
Over the inscribed slabs gulls rise and scream.
Singed petals scatter across the epitaphs.
The incoming sea's chopped white and green.

Orpheus' head churns in its own blood,
Shudders with each and every turbulence;
Battered, blind, it turns; bobs on the flood:
A severed head that will not sink,
But through the silence and the blood-stained rings
It sings - it sings - it sings - it sings - it sings.

IV

AFFAIRS OF THE HEART

The least things in the universe must be secret mirrors to the greatest
De Quincey

I

Love's Lexicon

Love has the gift of tongues; polyphony of words.
Our breath's cut short with each bright plosive
To flow again on sibilants. And **this,**
Love says, and **this,** and **this;** these eyes, these lips -
Adamic naming of the universe:
Our late night transformational grammar.
We lock together to ride the darkness
Until we drown in sleep.
I wake to witness
Love again. She's active in this place -
All instinct. As we stretch each limb,
Her hungry lexicon is at our lips.
You draw me to yourself and guide me in.
Her grammar's ours. It comes through broken gasps.
The morning sun is moist upon the glass.

II

Ungratified Desire

My dear child, how the hell can I live
With you on my knee, howling from colic
Or Kleinian breasts that never give -
Or whatever. And where's the help of William Blake? -
What is it men in women do require?
The lineaments of gratified desire.
What is it women do in men require.
The lineaments of gratified desire. -
When at every word I read you caterwaul,
God-knows-why for God-knows-what! Days
Now, I've wanted to make love. I call
Upon the testimony of Blake. I earn one kiss -
And then each time, dear child, you wake and yell
Desperate for those lovely, swollen breasts as well.

III

The Ancestral Voyage

Tonight rain clouds hang over Morfa Mawr,
Stranded whale which slopes into the bay
Of Cardiganshire. Against the dry stone wall
Our long Welsh house rests like a boat - each small
Window signals amber - now ready to float
Out on the incoming, gradual, tide of night.
Already our two daughters are asleep.
Their feet, like cut quartz, jut from the sheets;
Blond hair tangled in a galaxy of stars.
Our small son jerks his wrinkled hands, stirs
Momentarily. Murmurs. Returns to dream
The ancestral voyage. I perform last rites;
Top up the falling fire, wind the clock's
Dead weights, slide the bolt across the door,
And slowly come to you. My love, once more.

IV

Intentionality

We must define thought in terms of that strange power which it possesses of being ahead of itself, of launching itself and being at home everywhere.
Merleau Ponty

What, you ask, is intentionality?
Consider our new-born child. A bundle
Of cuddled flesh, barely a fledgling, yet
Between sucks darting into your doting eyes -
To return, elated after so much flying!
Or take the flight of birds. How by native powers
The mallard migrates, shakes its mottled wings
To the distant syntax of the stars.
Or take the cormorant, neck stretched low
To the incoming tide. How its beak, its eyes,
Cleave the future into which it flies.
What, you ask, is intentionality?
We arch forwards into time. By our intentions
Live out of reach. And, out of reach, retrieve ourselves.

V

Brechfa Garden

I might have taken a photograph of you
Just now, kneeling in Brechfa's garden,
Holding up the new root of gypsophila,
Its limp limbs lifeless after so long a journey;
A slim goddess hovering above her mandrake,
Framed by the wall I built, pear trees we staked -
But such a picture would have been half fake;
An image for nostalgic evenings.
It would not have illustrated what we know: -
How further down, beneath reaching of the spade,
Nettle and couch mat and burrow;
Lie ready to encroach upon this garden:
Paths, walls, shrubs, trees, borders - order
We for five years, together, laboured for.

VI

Fear before the Sacred Garden

See how the couple tread with caution -
For they intrude upon this garden where
All living species move through fire to fire,
Scarring the dumb earth, scorching the air.
See how in this uncompromising place
Even the cedar is half-conflagration -
The matted boughs crack and flare with spikes
Of light so sharp they end all concentration.
There is a meaning in their sombre dress,
The suburban lady's dark oppressive clothes;
Even the hat may form some kind of shield
Against the daemonic sun's hot hammer-blows.
Then are they wrong to turn, quickly retire
From this garden of apocalyptic fire?

VII

Estranged

And now we spend our lives staring through
These windows, streaming with rain, salt-stained.
Out where we look little's to be understood;
The wind contorts the jagged hawthorn bush.
Its clustered berries bleed into the wood.
In the smudged glass the farm's barn is shorn
Away. The field's flanged ruts reveal
Few variations. . . . .Tonight above the house
A battered moon drifts through the sky. It seeks
A pool, a mountain lake, in which to dip
Its scarred, distended cheeks, its frozen face.
Who, if not us, will warm this ice-cold child?
We argue. We touch. Refrain. Argue again.
Turn to sleep. Toss restlessly. Back to back.

VIII

Sunday Morning Aesthetic

You sit at the edge of the table, nude; your flesh
So finely stretched the ribs and bones show through.
African girl I come to you through CD
Players, Mozart's arias, Beaujolais Nouveau;
Our Sunday morning aesthetic. You gaze
Wide-eyed at us, part of the Sabbath's kill:
A snap, a shot buried between CITROEN AX
And KAWASAKI ZX10. You look at us;
Having nothing to sell or to display
You are the pitiless zero from which we rise.
Behind your body and your staring eyes
The shutters are almost closed against the day.

Outside on the suburban lawn the starlings preen,
Pick their gaudy wings. Strut. And gleam.

IX

Bad Times

The family thrives - but we divide time
Between Simenon and sleeping pills;
Our daughters, wide-eyed, flare through the house.
Play punk. Pout. Shout. Take possession.
They gaze in mirrors, lie without a blink,
Grab your underwear, grin, evaporate.
We move cautiously, avoid reflecting
Surfaces, keep cool, convey their messages.
Upstairs I struggle to thaw iced words;
You empty slops, iron, wash and shop.
Tranquillised we glide through Safeways, ghosts
Of our former selves. We wheel an empty box
Through frozen flesh and pyramids of tin -
Too far gone to see the hell we're in.

X

Love's Battleground

How in this warring marriage to survive
Love's battleground? We drag through the detritus
Of our own making. In the debris
Nothing grafts or roots or grows between us.
Terrorists we alter tack from hour to hour.
Your eyes open like blades. They're quick to cut.
My mouth is loaded with words. They aim to kill.
This is a prolonged and quite immoral war.
We suspect each other; read for duplicity,
Expect the worst. Emotions crash through our negotiations:
Escaped children, patients, war-lords - all of them crazy.
Our apprehensive looks are their exhausted faces.
Now, for no reason, there's a reversal of mood.
We're kissing like adolescent kids.
An interlude.

XI

Poor Icons

And sleepless at night, he saw his life passing
As on film. (The path went to the centre pond -
the kitchen garden was lemon in light -
but there were no voices - there was no laughter -
then they were together in Bath - city
of warm stone - arm in arm they strolled -
or sat turning the pages of the *Ravenna Mosaics* -
the saints' faces were lapped - and lit - with gold.)
And during the day he raided the drawer of jumbled
Photographs. Each spontaneous face, each lost event
Clamoured for a name, a place, a certain date.
Poor icons, I place them round the living-room.
Faded. Stained. Torn. A temenos of images
Plucked, a moment now, from transience.

XII

After the Storm

The night sky's cut with surging verticals
Of hail. At the far end of the garden
Spurred by gusts of wind, the sycamores
Rear all ways. Their manes are jagged green.
Lit up by zig-zag lightning small cloud wisps
Twist through the dark, downwards into nothingness.
We huddle close to each other. Precarious,
In this cosmic row our differences are less;
Our culminating points are gone in thunderclaps,
Inconsequential gasps before the flood.
The sky-stones rattle white into the foliage.
Ice-cold, the hail melts in our sticky palms.
We sense the reciprocity of living things.
The driven seeds are moist upon our flesh.

XIII

It Mends

Friends' marriages fray and break. Ours remains.
We grip the separate strands. Our hands are sore.
Love at times is minimal; it says, *Hold on*
And as the time runs out says nothing more.
The age conspires against the constant mind;
It puffs *Alternatives. New life-styles. State*
Of ultimate fulfilment, never specified.
And one is tempted to let what's been disintegrate.
Yet we hold on. Our hands are tested instruments.
These new grazes are slight against the weathered skin.
The rope has burnt into our palms;
And now we take the ends and tie them in.
Lying between us, it repairs. It takes and bears
The weight, the specific gravity of our lives.

V

MOVING OUT

For all ego-consciousness is isolated; it separates and discriminates, knows only particulars and sees only what can be related to the ego. Its essence is limitation, though it reaches to the furthest nebulae among the stars.
Anais Nin

I

Starting again

Momentarily a shadow rises on the rocks.
Then, as darkness devours the light, is gone.
A loose pebble leaps its scree. And drops.
Somewhere, blind bolts of water thunder down;
A crystal snaps and shivers the labyrinth -
Noise without narrative, sound without sense:
An ibex rears. A bison mounts. A muzzle shudders -
Lost to memory in the lapse of tense.
And then it starts. And starts again. In the dark
A hand rises up; splays out, imprints itself.
Flat *mappa mundi;* high on the rock,
Dripping ochre and white, stark sign of the self.
The lines materialize. The palm's pressure.
A map. To be read at desperate leisure.

II

Excavation

This sort of archaeology depends on the careful peeling off of successive thin layers of earth over a large area. In this way the team progress step by step towards the original surface. They move down five centimetres at a time and as they go down they are, of course, going further and further back in time.

Richard Leakey

Down. And further down. Back. And back -
What I seek is so distant, buried so
Far down under the thin tissues of black
Sediment, under the bric-a-brac, below
The charred pathologies of bone;
Down through the streaming lava flow
Of things, petrified: pots, beads, cut stone,
Ochre, ikon, pollen, sheer debris - slow
Recalcitrant clues to another's living;
Down through the shards of crumbling years,
Remorseless archaeologist, peeling
Back, one by one, the eluding surfaces -
Mad to grasp in this god-forsaken place
Minute fragments of the primordial face.

III

Via Negativa

Once there had been this God. He melted on
My tongue. Mind, mouth sealed, I sighed. I would
Preserve the taste of Him until the end
Of time! I pressed my palms against my eyes
Wanting the light more incandescent for
The darkness. A gawky teenager, not
Of his age, a cauldron of overheated
Appetites, desirous of martyrdom.
Still at the brink of things, restless, addicted
To more than life can yield, I set myself
To learn subtraction in this Edwardian home -
Where the unseen worm mines the antique wood.
There are small heaps of dust in every room.

I'm haunted by my own ingratitude.

IV

At the Extremities

This evening, under the tumultuous cloud, stubble
Burns, cracks and smoulders; the fields are stark
Rectangles of death; flints in rubble
And furrow; outstrips of chalk in the dark.
Persephone drifts here,
Singed poppies limp in her scarlet dress,
Her drugged mind driven near
The sudden gap in things where Hades is.
And Tolstoy, restless, to the end
Passionate for horizons, tracked by cameramen;
At the last station of his half-cracked mind
Whispering: 'I must go on. I must go on'.
And now a crescent moon drifts over the Downs -
Brief sign above glimmering boundaries.

V

After Faith

For some years I could not see. First faith
And faith's intensity blotted out my sight.
Then the ideal came. It spread a cataract
Across my eyes. Its harsh and minute scale
Became the boundary of a guarded world.
It blocked out the variegated life of things.
These summer fields, this mist, the tidal Ouse
Which slowly snakes through two chalk hills.
Prisoner of a paradox, I could not see
Through what I saw. My eyes were boarded in.
Today I head for Nature's holes and gaps.
My mind's out there, coinciding with whatever moves
Or simply is. Clouds merge with the evening haze.
The river's a small 's' between two mists.

VI

The Buddha Statue

On the Downs they are burning the stubble;
Across the fields smoke clouds rise and billow.
Stalks and husks are being burnt to dust -
Even the last thin silk poppies have to go,
Surrender their scarlet to the black. I linger
At the edges, to turn the cold dank shards
Of memory, to word a further question.
Yet on the mantlepiece the Buddha statue stands.
His crowned head is an infolded flower.
His slim body a stem in the jug of being.
His dark body glimmers.
All through the annihilating
Motion of this day his hands are still.
Time turns upon itself. And spirals in.

VII

Open to Change

Out from this rock, wind-worn, rain-razed
The Buddha stares into the bludgeoning storm;
The shrubs' roots crack open the dome of his mind;
The husks, bursting, break his woman's smile:
The death of the Buddha! And all patriarchs!
Yet he's composed; more tranquil now than when
His maker hacked him from intractable stone.
Soon blue butterflies will flit before him;
And ants will crawl across those worn eye-lids;
By his shoulders the leaves will burst their calyx
And unfold. Green. Yellow. Shrivel. And fade.
Beneath his gaze our lives betray themselves:
Broken, open to change. And the world turns
And turns. And the light burns. And the light burns.

VIII

Epilogue Poem: The Apple

Through open lips the paradox flows;
The clown's laughter is a refraction of sorrow.

In writing this I've half-erased my life.
I hear no voices. Have fewer memories now.
I buried a rectangular box last night.
The full moon was witness and participant.
After we had mourned my loss together
She moved on, a face, between the stars.
It was the clearest night I've ever known. Not a cloud.

I am what I apprehend.
What I have struggled with is who I am.

The cooling air eddies at my finger tips.
The apple on this branch is not yet picked,
Touched by moonlight, before perception split.